SO-ARM-361

HISTORY FROM OBJECTS
KEEPING
CLEAN

Karen Bryant-Mole

Wayland

HISTORY FROM OBJECTS

In The Home
Keeping Clean
At School
Toys
Clothes
In The Street

This edition published in 1996 by
Wayland (Publishers) Ltd

First published in 1994 by Wayland (Publishers) Ltd
61 Western Road, Hove, East Sussex, BN3 1JD, England

© Copyright 1994 Wayland (Publishers) Ltd

Edited by Deborah Elliott
Designed by Malcolm Walker

British Library Cataloguing in Publication Data
Bryant-Mole, Karen
    Keeping Clean. - (History From Objects Series)
    I. Title II. Series
    648.09

HARDBACK ISBN 0-7502-1022-2

PAPERBACK ISBN 0-7502-1897-5

Typeset by Kudos Editorial and Design Services
Printed and bound by BPC Paulton Books Ltd

Notes for parents and teachers
This book has been designed to be used on many different levels.

It can be used as a means of comparing and contrasting objects from the past with those of the present. Differences between the objects can be identified. Such differences might include the shape, colour or size of the objects.

It can be used to look at the way designs have developed as our knowledge and technology have improved. Children can consider the similarities between the objects and look at the way particular design features have been refined. They can look at the materials that the objects are made of and the way they work. Modern goods are often made of modern materials such as plastic. Older mechanical objects are now frequently powered by electricity.

The book can be used to help place objects in chronological order and to help children understand that development in design corresponds with a progression through time.

It can also be used to make deductions about the way people in the past lived their lives. Children can think about how and why the objects might have been used and who might have used them.

It is designed to show children that historical objects can reveal much about the past. At the same time it links the past with the present by showing that many of the familiar objects we use today have their roots firmly planted in history.

Contents

Some of the more difficult words which appear in **bold** are explained in the glossary on page 30.

Irons

Irons are used to press **creases** out of clothes.

1890s
This is a flat iron.
It was put on the range
to heat up. The iron got cold quickly,
so, two irons would have been used.
One iron would be heating up while
the other was being used.

1910s
Hot **charcoal** was placed in the box
on top of this iron to heat it up.
The iron stayed
hot for up to an hour.

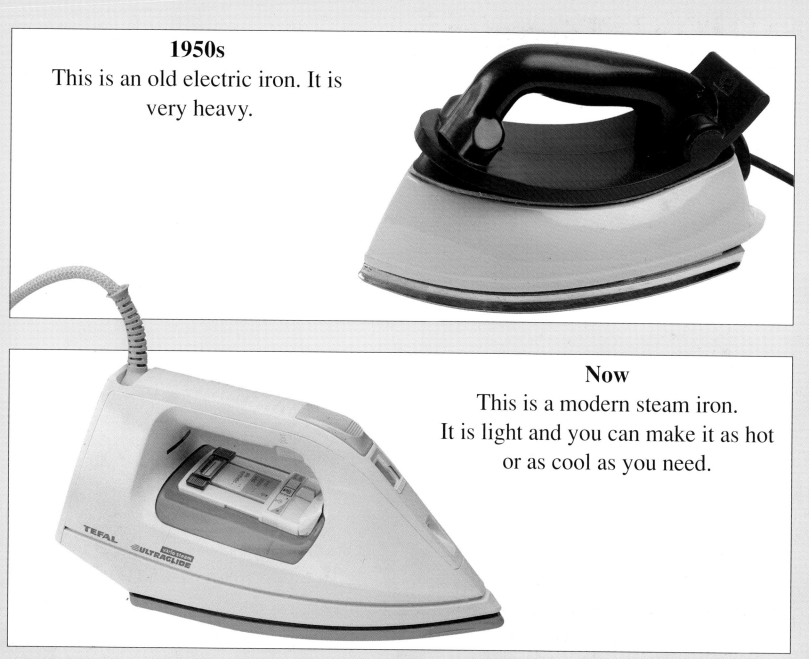

1950s
This is an old electric iron. It is
very heavy.

Now
This is a modern steam iron.
It is light and you can make it as hot
or as cool as you need.

Washing machines

We clean our clothes in washing machines.

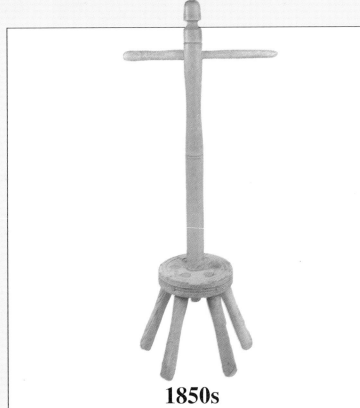

1850s

This wooden washing dolly was placed in a washing tub. It was twisted backwards and forwards to clean the clothes.

1860s

Here is a copper dolly. When the dolly was pushed up and down in the tub, the water squirted out through the holes in the side.

1930s

When the handle on the lid of this washing machine was turned, the paddle inside twisted about in the water and moved the clothes around.

Now

The washing machines we use today wash, rinse and spin. Some even dry our clothes too.

Washing powders

We use washing powders to get the dirt out of our clothes.

1920s

Before powders, people bought big blocks of washing soap. The blocks of soap were rubbed on to the clothes.

1940s

People could buy washing flakes, washing granules and washing powder. Washing powder was often used to wash dishes as well as clothes.

Now

We use washing powders and washing liquids to clean our clothes. Many modern **fabrics** come in bright colours, so special powders have been made to stop the colours fading.

Vacuum cleaners

We use vacuum cleaners to suck up dust from floors and carpets.

1880s
This is called
a dust pump.
The handle was
pumped up and
down and the dust
was sucked inside.

1900s
This vacuum cleaner
could be worked either
by electricity or
by hand by turning the
handle on the wheel at
the side. It must have
been hard work moving
this vacuum cleaner
around the house!

1940s

This Hoover vacuum cleaner has an advertisement on it:
IT BEATS AS IT SWEEPS AS IT CLEANS.

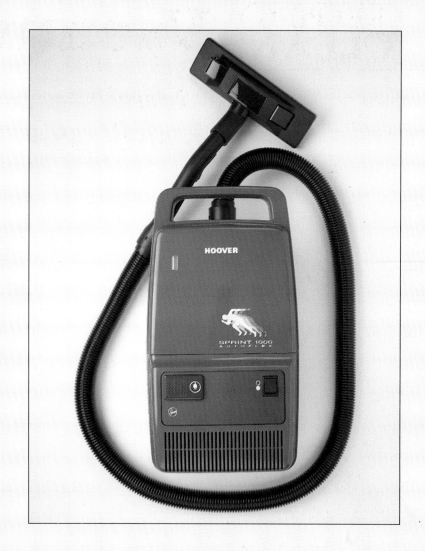

Now

Modern vacuum cleaners are light and easy to move around.

Hair wavers and dryers

People have often tried to make their hair curly.

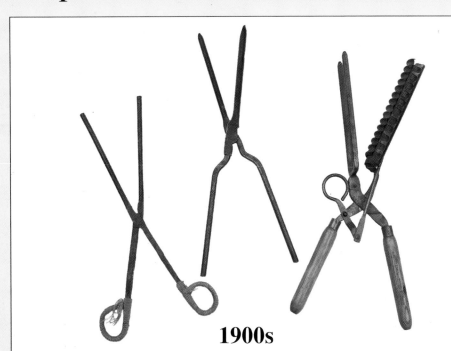

1900s
Here are some wavers and tongs which were used to curl hair. They were heated up on the range and then the hair was put between the tongs.

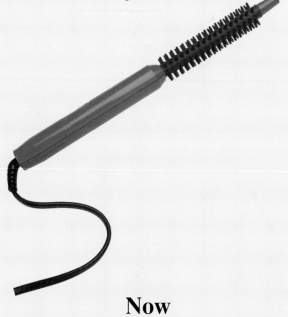

Now
Today's hair wavers use the same idea of wrapping the hair around something hot. Now the heat is usually made by electricity or gas.

We use hair dryers to dry our hair quickly.

1940s

Air is sucked in from the back of the hair dryer. The air is warmed up as it goes through a small heater and then the warm air is blown out through the nozzle at the front.

Now

The hair dryers we use today work in the same way. But we can make our hair dryers as warm or cool as we wish. This hair dryer is called a diffuser. Warm air comes out through lots of small holes.

Hair care

There are lots of different oils, shampoos, mousses and sprays we can use to make our hair look good.

1920s - 1930s

Men used oils to flatten their hair and make it look shiny. They used hair cream too, which made hair shine but wasn't as greasy as oil. Women used setting lotions with curlers to make straight hair curly. Can you see a bar of hair soap in the photograph? Before shampoo, people used to wash their hair with soap.

Now

Today there are even more things we can buy to look after our hair. We can choose from lots of different shampoos. We can dye our hair to make it lighter or darker. There are conditioners to make our hair shine. There are mousses and gels and sprays which keep our hair in place.

Ready for bed

What do you do before getting into bed each night?
You probably clean your teeth and wash your face.

1920s - 1950s

Toothpaste used to come in **stoneware** pots.
It was a very thick paste.
The hairbrush in the photograph has a wooden
handle. The picture on the box of soaps shows one
of the ways in which women used to style their
hair. The powdered bath cubes would have
made the bath water smell nice.

16

Now

The toothpaste we use today comes in **plastic** tubes.
The toothpaste is squeezed on to a plastic toothbrush.
Soap comes in all shapes and colours.

Do you use bubble bath? It can make bath time fun!
We use talcum powder, just like in the 1920s - 1950s, but now it comes in all kinds of fun **packaging.**

Shaving

Most men shave their faces every day.

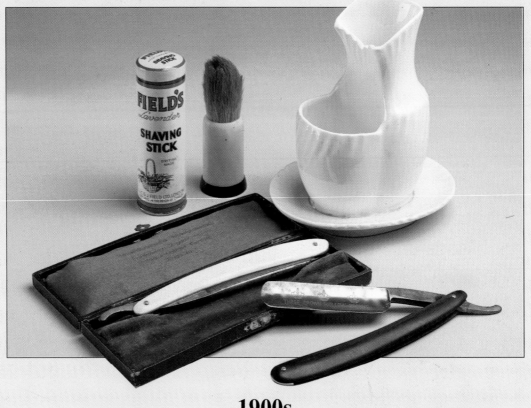

1900s

Shaving soap was put on with the shaving brush. The sharp blade on the razor was pulled across the face and this cut off the hair close to the skin. This type of razor was sometimes called a cut-throat razor. It sounds dangerous, doesn't it?

1940s

This is called a safety razor. The sharp blade was set inside a metal case. It was safer and easier to use than the cut-throat razor.

Now

This razor has a thin metal sheet with lots of tiny holes in it. The hair is cut by blades underneath this sheet of metal.

Kitchen sinks

We wash up dishes, glasses, knives, forks, spoons and pans in kitchen sinks.

1900s

This sink is made of stoneware.
It is coated with a **glaze**, which makes
the sink quite easy to clean.
The sink has a wooden draining board
for the clean dishes.

1970s

Here is a sink made of stainless steel.
It was easy to clean and, as the name
suggests, it did not stain in the same
way that earlier sinks did.

Now

Sinks today come in lots of colours and are made of many different materials. Instead of having two taps, one for hot water and one for cold water, this sink has a mixer tap. Both hot and cold water come out of a mixer tap.

Baths

We wash ourselves all over in baths.

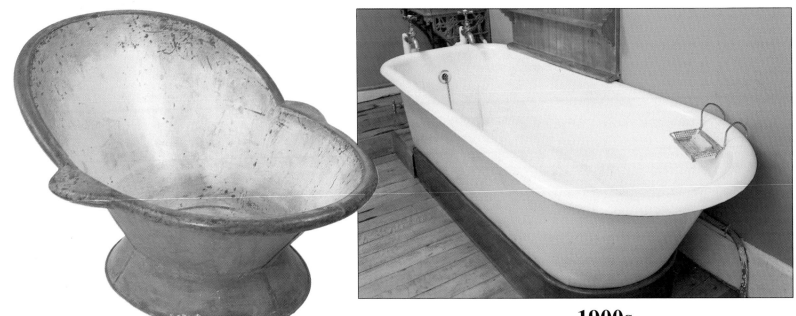

1840s -1930s

Bath tubs like this were put in front
of the fire and filled with water
heated on the range.
This type of bath is called a hip bath.
It looks small, doesn't it?

1900s

This is one of the first baths to be
in a bathroom.
It is made of metal painted
with enamel. Enamel is a special
sort of paint that doesn't crack
when it gets hot.

Now

This bath is made of a very strong plastic.

Modern baths come in lots of different colours, shapes and sizes.

This bath is very special - if you press a button the bath water gets all bubbly!

Wash basins

We wash our hands and faces in wash basins.

1880s

Before houses had hot running water, the water had to be heated on the range and brought to washing bowls in jugs.
This wash stand could be carried around.
The bowl and jug are made of tin coated with enamel.

24

1910s
This wash basin is made of
earthenware.
The basin is resting
on a stand made from cast iron.

Now
This wash basin has a pop-up
plug instead of a plug and chain.
It has only one tap.
You change the heat by
moving the **lever.**

Toilets

We sometimes call toilets, loos or lavatories.

1870s
This is called a boxed toilet.
It was **flushed** by pulling up
and pushing down on the handle in the little hole
next to the toilet bowl.

1880s

This toilet has a wooden seat. The tank where the water would have been kept was high above the bowl of the toilet. To flush the toilet you had to pull a handle on the end of a chain.

Now

Toilets now come in lots of different colours. In modern bathrooms the bath, wash basin, and toilet are often the same colour.

Cleaning boxes, polishes and cleaners

People have always had to clean their homes and the objects in their homes.

1900s

This is a wooden **grate** box. It held everything that was needed to clean the grate and the **hearth**. The gloves are made of cotton.

Now

The polishes and cleaners we use today are often kept in plastic boxes. The gloves are made of plastic too.

1900s

Here are some of the polishes and cleaners that might have been used over ninety years ago. There are powders for cleaning steps and hearths. There is some knife polish, some metal polish and a powder that seems to clean everything!

Now

Today's polishes and cleaners are made to care for the objects we use in our homes. There are cleaners for plastic baths, electric kettles, worktops and ovens. But one of the polishes from the 1900s is still used today and is in both photographs. Can you spot it?

Glossary

charcoal black, partly burnt wood

creases lines, folds or wrinkles

earthenware baked clay or pottery

fabrics materials that have been woven, such as cotton

flush to clean with a rush of water

glaze a see-through coating on pottery

grate a basket made of metal bars which is part of a fireplace

hearth the floor of a fireplace

lever a straight bar which can be moved

packaging the boxes and containers which things are sold in

stoneware a type of pottery

1840s	1850s	1860s	1870s	1880s	1890s	1900s	1910s

Books to read

History From Photographs series by Kath Cox and Pat Hughes (Wayland, 1995-6)
How We Used To Live, 1902-1926 by Freda Kelsall (A & C Black, 1985)
How We Used To Live, 1954-1970 by Freda Kelsall (A & C Black, 1987)
People Through History series by Karen Bryant-Mole (Wayland, 1996)
Starting History series by Stewart Ross (Wayland, 1991)

The illustration below is a timeline. The black and white drawings are of all the objects you have seen photographed in this book. Use the timeline to work out which objects came earlier or later than others, and which were around at the same time.

1920s	1930s	1940s	1950s	1960s	1970s	1980s	now

Index

Acknowledgements

The Publishers would like to thank the following organizations, which supplied the objects used in this book: By courtesy of the Royal Pavilion, Art Gallery and Museums (Preston Manor), Brighton 4 (both), 6 (right), 10 (left, middle), 12 (left), 20 (left), 22 (both), 24, 25 (top), 27 (left), 28 (left), 29 (top); Buckley's Yesterday's World, Battle, East Sussex 7 (left), 8 (both), 11 (left), 14, 16, 26; Barrett Southern Counties Limited 23, 25 (bottom), 27 (right); Norfolk Museums Service 18. All photographs are by Zul Mukhida except for page 18, which is by GGS Photographics.